STARTING TODAY...

365 quotations to stimulate, inspire, and enhance your personal growth.

Arranged By: Erika E. Gilchrist

© **MMVII** All rights reserved.

*A Gift to You
Compliments Of:*

JAN 1

"Each of us are angels with just one wing, and we can fly only by embracing each other."

-Unknown

JAN 2

"Complaining is proof that we haven't taken the time to find something to appreciate about ourselves or about anything in our lives."

-Anthony L. Gantt

JAN 3

"To improve is to change; to be perfect is to change often."

-Winston Churchill

JAN 4

"Energy and patience in business are two indispensable elements of success."

-P.T. Barnum

JAN 5

Intellectuals, like fish, often move in schools following a leader."

-Israel Shenker

JAN 6

"I am more and more convinced that our happiness or unhappiness depends far more on the way we meet the events of life than on the nature of those events themselves."

-Humboldt

JAN 7

"Service is the rent we pay for our place on earth."

-Alfred Armand Montapert

JAN 8

"People are always ready to admit a man's ability after he gets there."

-Confucius

JAN 9

"It is better to die on your feet than to live on your knees."

-Dolores Ibarruri

JAN 10

"Though humility is a virtue, an affected one is none."

-Anonymous

JAN 11

"What flows from your mouth can be the cause of depression and gloom, or your greatest source of contentment."

-Dale Carnegie Bronner

JAN 12

"To thine own Self be true, and it must follow, as the night the day. Thou canst not then be false to any man."

-William Shakespeare

JAN 13

"It is better to wear out than to rust out."

-Richard Cumberland

JAN 14

"The only place where success comes before work is a dictionary."

-Vidal Sassoon

JAN 15

"The ultimate measure of a man is not where he stands in moments of comfort, but where he stands at times of challenge and controversy."

- Dr. Martin Luther King, Jr.

JAN 16

"Great minds have purposes; others have wishes."

-Washington Irving

JAN 17

"Life is either a daring adventure or nothing at all."

-Helen Keller

JAN 18

"You want to be cautious when subscribing to the ideas of others, but the good news is that subscriptions can be cancelled."

-Erika Gilchrist

JAN 19

"Truth is scary; I guess that's why they say ignorance is bliss."

-Jessie Hault

JAN 20

"Doing the job RIGHT the first time gets the job done. Doing the job WRONG fourteen times gives you job security."

-Unknown

JAN 21

"It's quite unfortunate that a people who were once denied the right to read, only to overcome that challenge, are now regressing on their own will to be uneducated."

-Anonymous

JAN 22

"All know the way...few actually walk it."

-Bodhidharma

JAN 23

"Only those who risk going too far can possibly find out how far one can go."

-Eliot

JAN 24

"Unfortunately, if worry has become your reflex, mountain-making is what you do best."

-Dr. Joseph J. Luciani

JAN 25

"I may not have gone where I intended to go, but I think I have ended up where I intended to be."

-Douglas Adams

JAN 26

"A person who aims at nothing will surely hit it."

-Anon

JAN 27

"You can complain because roses have thorns, or you can rejoice because thorns have roses."

-Ziggy

JAN 28

"Whether you believe you can do a thing or not, you are right."

-Henry Ford

JAN 29

"Until you value yourself, you won't value your time. Until you value your time, you will not do anything with it."

-M Scott Peck

JAN 30

"For all sad words of tongue or pen, the saddest are these: 'It might have been!'"

-John Greenleaf Whittier

JAN 31

"Fall seven times, get up eight."

-Japanese Proverb

FEB 1

"Forget regret, or life is yours to miss."

-Jonathan Larson

FEB 2

You can discover what your enemy fears most by observing the means he uses to frighten you."

-Eric Hoffer

FEB 3

"Life does not cease to be funny when people die any more than it ceases to be serious when people laugh."

-George Bernard Shaw

FEB 4

"One of the tests of leadership is the ability to recognize a problem before it becomes an emergency."

-Arnold Glasgow

FEB 5

"When I hear somebody sigh, 'Life is hard,' I am always tempted to ask, 'Compared to what?'"

-Sydney Harris

FEB 6

"I don't know the key to success, but the key to failure is to try to please everyone."

-Bill Cosby

FEB 7

"We have met the enemy and it is us."

-Walt Kelly

FEB 8

"You may be disappointed if you fail, but you are doomed if you don't try."

-Beverly Sills

FEB 9

"A lot of fellows nowadays have a B.A., M.D., or Ph.D. Unfortunately, they don't have a J.O.B."

-Fats Domino

FEB 10

"Many a man is praised for his reserve and so-called shyness when he is simply too proud to risk making a fool of himself."

-J.B. Priestley

FEB 11

"There is a price to pay for everything you learn-whether from the school of hard knocks or the university of adversity."

-Dale Carnegie Bronner

FEB 12

"Fear is that little darkroom where negatives are developed."

-Michael Pritchard

FEB 13

"The difference between a boss and a leader: a boss says, 'Go!' – a leader says, 'Let's go!'"

-E.M. Kelly

FEB 14

"You don't love a woman because she is beautiful, but she is beautiful because you love her."

-Anon

FEB 15

"Do not go where the path may lead. Go instead where there is no path and leave a trail."

-Emerson

FEB 16

"When you feel that you have reached the end and that you cannot go one step further, when life seems to be drained of all purpose: What a wonderful opportunity to start all over again, to turn over a new page."

-Eileen Caddy

FEB 17

"A lot of successful people are risk-takers. Unless you're willing to do that...to have a go, fail miserably, and have another go, success won't happen."

-Philip Adams

FEB 18

"As long as you accept only those limited thoughts that have been bred into you, you will never activate greater portions of your brain to receive and experience any thought other than what you have faced every day of your existence."

-Ramtha

FEB 19

"Let's start looking at people that do us wrong as people who are giving us the opportunity to share the love that we have within us."

-Anthony L. Gantt

FEB 20

"Most of us have an awful lot of information to share with people and the world. Please do not cheat people any longer."

-Dr. Cuttie Bacon, III

FEB 21

"The great act of faith is when man decides that he is not God."

-Oliver Wendell Holmes, Jr.

FEB 22

"Even if you're on the right track, you'll get run over if you just sit there."

-Will Rogers

FEB 23

"The ultimate question which every man has to face and answer for themselves is: Will you be a hero or a coward?"

William Ernest Hocking

FEB 24

"The ultimate leader is one who is willing to develop people to the point that they eventually surpass him or her in knowledge and ability."

-Fred A. Manske, Jr.

FEB 25

"The best way out is always through."

-Robert Frost

FEB 26

"In the middle of difficulty lies opportunity."

-Albert Einstein

FEB 27

"Much unhappiness has come into the world because of things left unsaid..."

-Dostoevsky

FEB 28

"The reason people blame things on the previous generation is that there's only one other choice."

-Doug Larson

FEB 29

"You cannot escape the responsibility of tomorrow by evading it today."

-Abraham Lincoln

MAR 1

"Not all who wander are lost."

-J.R. Tolkien

MAR 2

"Obstacles are those frightful things you see when you take your eyes off your goal."

-Henry Ford

MAR 3

"Honest disagreement is often a good sign of progress."

-Mahatma Gandhi

MAR 4

"No one has the right to destroy another person's belief by demanding empirical evidence."

-Ann Landers

MAR 5

"The central question in ANY decision is, "What would love do now?"

-Conversations With God: Book 2

MAR 6

"The supreme happiness of life is being loved for yourself, in spite of yourself."

-Victor Hugo

MAR 7

"The future depends on what we do in the present."

-Mahatma Gandhi

MAR 8

"The great man is he who does not lose his child's heart."

-Mencius

MAR 9

"Happiness resides not in possessions and not in gold; the feeling of happiness dwells in the soul."
-Democritus

MAR 10

"Keep steadily before you the fact that all true success depends at last upon yourself".-
Theodore T. Hunger

MAR 11

"I cannot believe that the purpose of life is to be happy. I think the purpose of life is to be useful, to be responsible, to be compassionate. It is, above all to matter, to count, to stand for something, to have made some difference that you lived at all."

-Leo Rosten

MAR 12

*"You gain strength, courage, and confidence by every experience in which you really stop to look fear in the face. You are able to say to yourself, 'I have lived through this horror. I can take the next thing that comes along.' . . . **You must do the thing you think you cannot do.**"*

-Eleanor Roosevelt

MAR 13

"You must be the change you wish to see in the world."

-Mahatma Gandhi

MAR 14

"Even though you may want to move forward in your life, you may have one foot on the brakes. In order to be free, we must learn how to let go. Release the hurt. Release the fear. Refuse to entertain your old pain. The energy it takes to hang onto the past is holding you back from a new life. What is it you would let go of today?"

-Mary Manin Morrissey

MAR 15

"The searching-out and thorough investigation of truth ought to be the primary study of man."
-Cicero

MAR 16

"What happens to a man is far less significant than what happens within him."
- Louis L. Mann

MAR 17

"One cannot think crooked and walk straight."
- unknown

MAR 18

"The grand essentials of happiness are: something to do, something to love, and something to hope for."

-Allan K. Chalmers

MAR 19

"Either you run the day or the day runs you."
-Jim Rohn

MAR 20

"If I am not for myself, who will be? And if I am for myself alone, then what am I? And if not now, when?"

-Rabbi Hillel, Pirke Avot 1:14

MAR 21

"It's not the size of the dog in the fight; it's the size of the fight in the dog."

-Mark Twain

MAR 22

"Avoiding the phrase 'I don't have time...', will soon help you to realize that you do have the time needed for just about anything you choose to accomplish in life."

-Bo Bennett

MAR 23

"All men dream, but not equally. Those who dream by night in the dusty recesses of their minds, wake in the day to find that it was vanity: but the dreamers of the day are dangerous men, for they may act on their dreams with open eyes, to make them possible."

-Thomas Edward Lawrence (of Arabia)

MAR 24

"Adversity is the first path to truth."

-George Gordon Byron

MAR 25

"If you don't like something, change it. If you can't change it, change your attitude. Don't complain."

-Maya Angelou

MAR 26

"We live in a moment of history where change is so speeded up that we begin to see the present only when it is already disappearing."

-R.D. Laing

MAR 27

"The most important of life's battles is the one we fight daily in the silent chambers of the soul.

- David O. McKay

MAR 28

"If you feel you have no faults ... there's another one."

- Unknown

MAR 29

"The main thing is to keep the main thing the main thing."
- Steven Covey

MAR 30

"You are never given a wish without also being given the power to make it true. You may have to work for it, however."
- Richard Bach

MAR 31

"Remember sadness is always temporary. This, too, shall pass."
-Chuck T. Falcon

APR 1

"The men who try to do something and fail are infinitely better than those who try to do nothing and succeed."
- Lloyd Jones

APR 2

"One hundred percent of the shots you don't take don't go in."
- Wayne Gretzky

APR 3

"The more often a man feels without acting, the less he'll be able to act. And in the long run, the less he'll be able to feel."

-C.S. Lewis

APR 4

"The quarrels of lovers are like summer storms; everything is more beautiful when they have passed."

-Madame Necker

APR 5

"What difference does it make how much you have? What you do not have amounts to much more."

-Seneca

APR 6

"Hope is like a bird that senses the dawn and carefully starts to sing while it is still dark."

-unknown

APR 7

"You never change things by fighting the existing reality. To change something, build a new model that makes the existing model obsolete."

-Buckminster Fuller

APR 8

"The most terrifying thing is to accept oneself completely."

-Carl Gustay Jung

APR 9

"Take rest; a field that has rested gives beautiful crop."

-Ovid

APR 10

"Winning starts with beginning."

- Robert Schuller

APR 11

"How much longer will you go on letting your energy sleep? How much longer are you going to stay oblivious of the immensity of yourself? Don't lose time in conflict; lose no time in doubt - time can never be recovered, and if you miss an opportunity it may take many lives before another comes your way again."

-Bhagwan Shree Rajneesh

APR 12

"Always feel free to express yourself. Don't worry about who you're going to offend because no matter how sincere your intentions may be, the moment you open your mouth you are guaranteed to have offended at least one person. In the end, after you've tried everything in the world to try not to offend the entire human race, you will have in fact offended yourself by not being yourself. Now that's offensive."

-Zernul Shackelford

APR 13

"The block of granite which was an obstacle in the pathway of the weak, became a stepping-stone in the pathway of the strong."

-Thomas Carlyle

APR 14

"Most of us have an awful lot of information to share with people and the world. Please do not cheat people any longer."

-Cutty W. Bacon III

APR 15

"Procrastination is the thief if time."

-Edward Young

APR 16

"The future opens up before you like a new book...waiting for you to commit to its pages the story only you can write."

-Book: No Limits But The Sky

APR 17

"If I had a formula for bypassing trouble, I would not pass it round. Trouble creates a capacity to handle it."

-Oliver Wendell Holmes

APR 18

"Nothing would be done at all if a man waited until he could do it so well that no-one could find fault with it."

-Cardinal Newman

APR 19

"What would you attempt to do if you knew you could not fail?"

-Dr. Robert Schuller

APR 20

"Life is what happens to us while we are making other plans."

-Thomas La Mance

APR 21

"Only dread one day at a time."

-Charles Schultz

APR 22

"My grandfather always said that living is like licking honey off a thorn."

-Louis Adamic

APR 23

"It is only possible to live happily ever after on a day to day basis."

-Margaret Bonnano

APR 24

"There is nothing noble in being superior to some other men; the true nobility is in being superior to your previous self."

-Hindu proverb

APR 25

"Men stumble over pebbles, never over mountains."

-Anonymous

APR 26

"Dost thou wish to rise? Begin by descending."

-Saint Augustine

APR 27

"To go too far is as bad as to fall short."

-Confucius

APR 28

"In great attempts it is glorious even to fail."

-Cassius Longinus

APR 29

"It is not what he has, nor even what he does, which directly expresses the worth of a man, but what he is."

-Henri-Frederic Amiel

APR 30

"Belief consists in accepting the affirmations of the soul; unbelief in denying them."

-Ralph Waldo Emerson

MAY 1

"Say not, when I have leisure I will study; you may not have leisure."

-The Mishnah

MAY 2

"I would rather be adorned by beauty of character than by jewels. Jewels are the gift of fortune, while comes from within."

-Plautus

MAY 3

""Always laugh when you can; it is a cheap medicine. It is the sunny side of existence."

-George Gordon Byron

MAY 4

"Conscience is a thousand witnesses."

-Ancient Proverb

MAY 5

"Courage conquers all things; it even gives strength to the body."

-Ovid

MAY 6

"I had rather be defeated in a cause that will ultimately triumph than triumph in a cause that will ultimately be defeated."

-Woodrow Wilson

MAY 7

"It is much more difficult to overcome a bad habit, than it is to form a new one."

-Mary Wright Weaver

MAY 8

"The most complete revenge is not to imitate the aggressor."

-Marcus Aurelius

MAY 9

"It is not poverty that we praise, it is the man whom poverty cannot humble or bend."

-Seneca

MAY 10

"Faith is the bird that sings when the dawn is still dark."

-Sir Rabindranath Tagore

MAY 11

"The only failure a man ought to fear is failure in cleaving to the purpose he sees best."

-George Eliot

MAY 12

"People are often lonely because they build walls instead of bridges."

-Anonymous

MAY 13

"The true spirit of conversation consists in building on another man's observation, not overturning it."

-Edward Bulwer-Lytton

MAY 14

"Nothing is more scandalous than a man who is proud of his humility."

-Marcus Aurelius

MAY 15

"He that gives should never remember, he that receives should never forget."

-The Talmud

MAY 16

"If there is a scarcity of happiness in the world, it is because more people try to share it than produce it."

-Anonymous

MAY 17

"Friendship is one mind in two bodies."

-Mencius

MAY 18

"He who forgives ends the quarrel."

-African Proverb

MAY 19

"One hour of justice is worth a hundred of prayer."

Arab Proverb

MAY 20

"Not to aid one in distress is to kill him in your heart."

-African Proverb

MAY 21

"If you have knowledge, let others light their candles by it."

-Margaret Fuller

MAY 22

"It is often easier to fight for principles than to live up to them."

-Adlai E. Stevenson

MAY 23

"Nothing is so strong as gentleness, nothing as gentle as real strength."

-Saint Francis De Sales

MAY 24

"Choose a job that you like and you will not have to work a day in your life."

-Confucius

MAY 25

"Define irony: rush hour is that hour when traffic is almost at a standstill."

-J.B. Morton

MAY 26

"Tact is the art of convincing people that they know more than you do."

-Raymond Mortimer

MAY 27

"When money speaks the truth is silent."

-Anonymous

MAY 28

"Everything comes those who hustles while he waits."

-Thomas Edison

MAY 29

"I was brought up to respect my elders and now I don't have to respect anybody."

-George Burns

MAY 30

"men who never get carried away should be."

-Malcolm Forbes

MAY 31

"If you aren't fired with enthusiasm, you will be fired with enthusiasm."

-Vince Lombardi

JUN 1

"If you would not be forgotten as soon as you are dead, either write things worth reading or do things worth writing."

-Benjamin Franklin

JUN 2

"If you don't drive your business you will be driven out of business."

-B.C. Forbes

JUN 3

"Book lovers never go to bed alone."

-Daniel J Boorstin

JUN 4

"Adversity introduces people to themselves."

-Anonymous

JUN 5

"One thorn of experience is worth a whole wilderness of warning."

-James Russell Lowell

JUN 6

"If there were no clouds we would not enjoy the sun."

-Ancient Proverb

JUN 7

"The gem cannot be polished without friction, nor man perfected without trials."

-Chinese Proverb

JUN 8

"Old age to the unlearned is winter; to the learned, it is harvest time."

-Yiddish Proverb

JUN 9

"You cannot be anything if you want to be everything."

-Solomon Schechter

JUN 10

"I find that the great thing is not so much where we stand as in what direction we are moving."

-Anonymous

JUN 11

"Reflect upon your present blessings, of which every person has many; not on your past misfortunes, of which all people have only some."

-Charles Dickens

JUN 12

"Ah, summer, what power you have to make us suffer and like it."

-Hal Borland

JUN 13

"Character, like a kettle, once mended always requires repairs."

-Ancient Proverb

JUN 14

"Character is what you are in the dark."

-Dwight L Moody

JUN 15

"If we had no faults, we should not take so much pleasure in noting those of others."

-Francois La Rochefoucauld

JUN 16

"Gladness of the heart is the life of man, and the joyfulness of a man prolongeth his days."

-The Apocrypha

JUN 17

"It takes more than a soft pillow to insure a sound sleep."

-Anonymous

JUN 18

"Courage consists not so much in avoiding danger as in conquering it."

-Ancient Proverb

JUN 19

"The essence of optimism is that it takes no account of the present, but it is a source of inspiration, of vitality and hope where others have resigned; it enables a man to hold his head high, to claim the future for himself and not to abandon it to his enemy."

-Dietrich Bonhoeffer

JUN 20

"When I look into the future, it's so bright it burns my eyes."

-Oprah Winfrey

JUN 21

"We all live under the same sky, but we don't all have the same horizon."

-Konrad Adenauer

JUN 22

"To begin to think with purpose, is to enter the ranks of those strong ones who only recognize failure as one of the pathways to attainment."

-James Allen

JUN 23

"Life is not a having and a getting, but a being and a becoming."

-Matthew Arnold

JUN 24

"We must have a theme, a goal, a purpose in our lives. If you don't know where you're aiming, you don't have a goal. My goal is to live my life in such a way that when I die, someone can say, she cared."

-Mary Kay Ash

JUN 25

"Not all who wander are lost."

-J. R. R. Tolkien

JUN 26

"To come to be you must have a vision of Being, a Dream, a Purpose, a Principle. You will become what your vision is."

-Peter Nivio Zarlenga

JUN 27

"Failure is not reaching your goal, but in having no goal to reach."

-Benjamin Mays

JUN 28

"Far better it is to dare mighty things, to win glorious triumphs, even though checkered by failure, than to take rank with those poor spirits who neither enjoy much nor suffer much, because they live in the gray twilight that

knows not victory nor defeat."

-Theodore Roosevelt

JUN 29

"Adversity is the first path to truth."

-Lord (George Gordon) Byron

JUN 30

"Human potential, though not always apparent, is there waiting to be discovered and invited forth."

-William P Purkey

JUL 1

"Ability will never catch up with the demand for it."

-Malcolm Stevenson Forbes

JUL 2

"We don't know who we are until we see what we can do."

-Martha Grimes

JUL 3

"Ability may get you to the top, but it takes character to keep you there."

-John Wooden

JUL 4

"In America, if you put your mind to it you can have anything you want."

-Bernard Baruch

JUL 5

"It is easy to be brave from a safe distance."

-Aesop

JUL 6

"Optimism is the foundation of courage."

-Nicholas Murray Butler

JUL 7

"He who does not have the courage to speak up for his rights cannot earn the respect of others."

-René G. Torres

JUL 8

"The best executive is one who has sense enough to pick good people to do what he wants them to do, and self-restraint enough to keep from meddling with them while they do it."

-Theodore Roosevelt

JUL 9

"Wisdom is supreme; therefore make a full effort to get wisdom. Esteem her and she will exalt you; embrace her and she will honor you."

Proverbs 4: 7-8

JUL 10

"Integrity has no need of rules."

-Albert Camus

JUL 11

"Respect human talent, respond to genius, recognize reality, admire truth and beauty, realize the meaning of the rare flower Reason."

Peter Nivio Zarlenga

JUL 12

"You must be true to yourself. Strong enough to be true to yourself. Brave enough to be strong enough to be true to yourself. Wise enough to be brave enough to be strong enough to shape yourself from what you actually are."

Sylvia Ashton-Warner

JUL 13

"Other people's opinion of you does not have to become your reality."

-Les Brown

JUL 14

"Only the spoon knows what is stirring in the pot."

-Sicilian Proverb

JUL 15

"The most wasted day of all is that during which we have not laughed."

-Sebastian R. N. Chamfort

JUL 16

"Through zeal knowledge is gotten, through lack of zeal knowledge is lost; let a man who knows this double path of gain and loss thus place himself that knowledge may grow."

-Buddha

JUL 17

"Knowledge is an unending adventure at the edge of uncertainty."

-Jacob Bronowski

JUL 18

"The test of courage comes when we are in the minority.

-Ralph W. Sockman

JUL 19

"There are two things to aim at in life; first to get what you want, and after that to enjoy it. Only the wisest of mankind has achieved the second."

-Logan Pearsall Smith

JUL 20

"Motivation is what gets you started. Habit is what keeps you going."

-Jim Ryun

JUL 21

"Dream lofty dreams, and as you dream, so you shall become. Your vision is the promise of what you shall one day be; your ideal is the prophecy of what you shall at last unveil."

-James Allen

JUL 22

"A dream becomes a goal when action is taken toward its achievement."

-Bo Bennett

JUL 23

"When you get to the end of your rope, tie a knot and hang on."

-Franklin D Roosevelt

JUL 24

"America's future will be determined by the home and the school. The child becomes largely what he is taught; hence we must watch what we teach, and how we live."

-Jane Addams

JUL 25

"My riches consist not in the extent of my possessions, but in the fewness of my wants."

-Joseph Brotherton

JUL 26

"There's no reason to be the richest man in the cemetery. You can't do any business from there."

-Colonel Harland Sanders

JUL 27

"Before anything else, preparation is the key to success."

-Alexander Graham Bell

JUL 28

"I arise in the morning torn between a desire to save the world and a desire to savor the world. That makes it hard to plan the day."

-E.B. (Elwyn Brooks) White

JUL 29

"One cannot subdue a man by holding back his hands. Lasting peace comes not from force."

-David Borenstein

JUL 30

"Even as the cell is the unit of the organic body, so the family is the unit of society."

-Ruth Nanda Anshen

JUL 31

"To the outside world we all grow old. But not to brothers and sisters. We know each other as we always were. We know each other's hearts. We share private family jokes. We remember family feuds and secrets, family griefs and joys. We live outside the touch of time."

-Clara Ortega

AUG 1

"You can always cope with the present moment, but you cannot cope with something that is only a mind projection – you cannot recreate the past."

Elkhart Tolle

AUG 2

"People seldom refuse help, if one offers it in the right way."

-A. C. Benson

AUG 3

"If your energy is as boundless as your ambition, total commitment may be a way of life you should seriously consider."

-Joyce Brothers

AUG 4

"It is a denial of justice not to stretch out a helping hand to the fallen; that is the common right of humanity."

-Seneca (Seneca the Elder)

AUG 5

"A candle loses nothing by lighting another candle."

-Father James Keller

AUG 6

"Individual commitment to a group effort -- that is what makes a team work, a company work, a society work, a civilization work."

-Vince Lombardi

AUG 7

"You have brains in your head, you have feet in your shoes you can steer yourself in any direction you choose."

-Theodor Seuss Geisel (Dr. Seuss)

AUG 8

"Yes and no are very powerful words. Mean them when you say them. Respect them when you hear them."

-Michael Josephson

AUG 9

"It is the mark of an educated mind to be able to entertain a thought without accepting it."

-Aristotle

AUG 10

"The cynic never grows up, but commits intellectual suicide."

-Charles R. Brown

AUG 11

"The fact that I can plant a seed and it becomes a flower, share a bit of knowledge and it becomes another's, smile at someone and receive a smile in return, are to me continual spiritual exercises."

-Leo Buscaglia

AUG 12

"We are all spiritual beings having a human experience."

-Anon

AUG 13

"*Loyalty is still the same, whether it win or lose the game; True as a dial to the sun, although it be not shined upon.*"

-Samuel Butler (poet)

AUG 14

"*Time is a sort of river of passing events, and strong is its current; no sooner is a thing brought to sight than it is swept by and another takes its place, and this too will be swept away.*"

-Marcus Aurelius

AUG 15

"*The best way to pay for a lovely moment is to enjoy it.*"

-Richard Bach

AUG 16

"*Time is not a line, but a series of now-points*".

-Taisen Deshimaru

AUG 17

"*Time is too slow for those who wait, too swift for those who fear, too long for those who grieve, too short for those who rejoice, but for those who love, time is eternity. Hours fly, flowers die, new days, new ways pass by, love stays."

-Henry Van Dyke

AUG 18

"Do the thing you fear to do and keep on doing it... that is the quickest and surest way ever yet discovered to conquer fear."

-Dale Carnegie

AUG 19

"The difference between perseverance and obstinacy is, that one often comes from a strong will, and the other from a strong won't."

-Henry Ward Beecher

AUG 20

"Perseverance is the hard work you do after you get tired of doing the hard work you already did."

-Newt Gingrich

AUG 21

"He conquers who endures."

-Persius

AUG 22

"The real measure of your wealth is how much you'd be worth if you lost all your money."

-Anon

AUG 23

"Our faith in the present dies out long before our faith in the future."

-Ruth Benedict

AUG 24

"Big jobs usually go to the men who prove their ability to outgrow small ones."

-Ralph Waldo Emerson

AUG 25

"If we had no winter, the spring would not be so pleasant; if we did not sometimes taste of adversity, prosperity would not be so welcome."

-Anne Dudley Bradstreet

AUG 26

"No bird soars too high if he soars with his own wings."

-William Blake

AUG 27

"You can't build a reputation on what you're going to do."

-Henry Ford

AUG 28

"Ability is of little account without opportunity."

-Napoleon Bonaparte

AUG 29

"Doing the best at this moment puts you in the best place for the next moment."

-Oprah Winfrey

AUG 30

"Grace is but glory begun, and glory is but grace perfected."

-Jonathan Edwards

AUG 31

"The person with a fixed goal, a clear picture of his desire, or an ideal always before him, causes it, through repetition, to be buried deeply in his subconscious mind and is thus enabled, thanks to its generative and sustaining power, to realize his goal in a minimum of time and with a minimum of physical effort. Just pursue the thought unceasingly. Step by step you will achieve realization, for all your faculties and powers become directed to that end."

-Claude M. Bristol

SEP 1

"It's a heck of a start, being able to recognize what makes you happy."

-Lucille Ball

SEP 2

"Some people never find it, some only pretend, but I just want to live happily ever after every now and then."

-Jimmy Buffett

SEP 3

"Don't throw a drowning man a rope then refuse to pull him to shore."

-Conversations With God - Book 1

SEP 4

"Accept that all of us can be hurt, that all of us can -- and surely will at times -- fail. I think we should follow a simple rule: if we can take the worst, take the risk."

-Joyce Brothers

SEP 5

"And the day came when the risk it took to remain tight inside the bud was more painful than the risk it took to blossom."

-Anais Nin

SEP 6

"Not armies, not nations, have advanced the race; but here and there, in the course of ages, an individual has stood up and cast his shadow over the world."

-Edwin Hubbell Chapin

SEP 7

"Ideas pull the trigger, but instinct loads the gun."

-Don Marquis

SEP 8

"We forfeit three-fourths of ourselves in order to be like other people."

-Arthur Schopenhauer

SEP 9

"Since each person, as an individual, is the not-being of the other, it is never possible to eliminate non-understanding completely."

Friedrich Schleiermacher

SEP 10

"He who asks a question is a fool for five minutes; he who does not ask a question remains a fool forever."

-Chinese Proverb

SEP 11

"America is woven of many strands. I would recognize them and let it so remain. Our fate is to become one, and yet many."

-Ralph Ellison

SEP 12

'A book may be as great a thing as a battle."

-Benjamin Disraeli

SEP 13

"It is important that students bring a certain ragamuffin, barefoot, irreverence to their studies; they are not here to worship what is known, but to question it."

-Jacob Bronowski

SEP 14

"Aerodynamically, the bumble bee shouldn't be able to fly, but the bumble bee doesn't know it so it goes on flying anyway."

-Mary Kay Ash

SEP 15

"Take rest; a field that has rested gives a bountiful crop."

-Ovid

SEP 16

"We don't know who we are until we see what we can do."

-Martha Grimes

SEP 17

"As simple as it sounds, we all must try to be the best person we can: by making the best choices, by making the most of the talents we've been given."

-Mary Lou Retton

SEP 18

"We count our miseries carefully, and accept our blessings without much thought."

-Chinese Proverb

SEP 19

"Let us rise up and be thankful, for if we didn't learn a lot today, at least we learned a little, and if we didn't learn a little, at least we didn't get sick, and if we got sick, at least we didn't die; so, let us all be thankful."

-Buddha

SEP 20

"Can you see the holiness in those things you take for granted--a paved road or a washing machine? If you concentrate on finding what is good in every situation, you will discover that your life will suddenly be filled with gratitude, a feeling that nurtures the soul."

-Rabbi Harold Kushner

SEP 21

"My advice to you is not to inquire why or whither, but just enjoy your ice cream while it's on your plate."

-Thornton Wilder

SEP 22

"If a man be gracious and courteous to strangers, it shows he is a citizen of the world, and that his heart is no island cut off from other lands, but a continent that joins to them."

-Francis Bacon

SEP 23

"The fragrance always stays in the hand that gives the rose."

-Hada Bejar

SEP 24

"We make a living by what we get. We make a life by what we give."

-Sir Winston Churchill

SEP 25

"In poverty and other misfortunes of life, true friends are a sure refuge. The young they keep out of mischief; to the old they are a comfort and aid in their weakness, and those in the prime of life they incite to noble deeds."

-Aristotle

SEP 26

"Don't walk behind me; I may not lead. Don't walk in front of me; I may not follow. Just walk beside me and be my friend."

-Albert Camus

SEP 27

"To come to be you must have a vision of Being, a Dream, a Purpose, a Principle. You will become what your vision is."

-Peter Nivio Zarlenga

SEP 28

"If a man does not keep pace with his companions, perhaps it is because he hears a different drummer. Let him step to the music which he hears, however measured or far away."

-Henry David Thoreau

SEP 29

The victory of success is half won when one gains the habit of setting goals and achieving them. Even the most tedious chore will become endurable as you parade through each day convinced that every task, no matter how menial or boring, brings you closer to fulfilling your dreams.

-Og Mandino

SEP 30

"Give love and unconditional acceptance to those you encounter, and notice what happens."

-Wayne Dyer

OCT 1

"Wisdom begins in wonder."

-Socrates

OCT 2

*"Letters to absence can a voice impart,
And lend a tongue when distance gags the heart."*

-Horace Walpole

OCT 3

"Your only obligation in any lifetime is to be true to yourself. Being true to anyone else or anything else is...impossible."

-Richard Bach

OCT 4

"By three methods we may learn wisdom: First, by reflection, which is noblest; Second, by imitation, which is easiest; and third by experience, which is the bitterest."

-Confucius

OCT 5

"October is the fallen leaf, but it is also a wider horizon more clearly seen. It is the distant hills once more in sight, and the enduring constellations above them once again."

-Hal Borland

OCT 6

"Optimism doesn't wait on facts. It deals with prospects. Pessimism is a waste of time."

-Norman Cousins

OCT 7

"The nice part about being a pessimist is that you are constantly being either proven right or pleasantly surprised."

-George Will

OCT 8

"Everyone is kneaded out of the same dough but not baked in the same oven."

-Yiddish Proverb

OCT 9

"Just when you think that a person is just a backdrop for the rest of the universe, watch them and see that they laugh, they cry, they tell jokes ... they're just friends waiting to be made."

-Dr. Jeffrey Borenstein

OCT 10

"Most of the great triumphs and tragedies of history are caused not by people being fundamentally good or fundamentally evil, but by people being fundamentally people."

-Terry Pratchett

OCT 11

"If you come to a fork in the road, take it."

-Yogi Berra

OCT 12

"Life doesn't make any sense, and we all pretend it does. Comedy's job is to point out that it doesn't make sense, and that it doesn't make much difference anyway."

-Eric Idle

OCT 13

"Humor is a spontaneous, wonderful bit of an outburst that just comes. It's unbridled, it's unplanned, it's full of surprises."

-Erma Bombeck

OCT 14

*"Reason to rule but mercy to forgive:
The first is the law, the last prerogative."*

-John Dryden

OCT 15

"Tis nobler to lose honor to save the lives of men than it is to gain honor by taking them."

-David Borenstein

OCT 16

"Fall seven times, stand up eight."

-Japanese Proverb

OCT 17

" Man never made any material as resilient as the human spirit."

-Bernard Williams

OCT 18

"In retrospect, the past seems not one existence with a continuous flow of years and events that follow each other in logical sequence, but a life periodically dividing into entirely

separate compartments. Change of surroundings, interests, pursuits, has made it seem actually more like different incarnations."

-Eleanor Robson Belmont

OCT 19

"The unexamined life is not worth living."

-Socrates

OCT 20

"Knowledge of the self is the mother of all knowledge. So it is incumbent on me to know my self, to know it completely, to know its minutiae, its characteristics, its subtleties, and its very atoms."

-Kahlil Gibran

OCT 21

"The trouble with so many of us is that we underestimate the power of simplicity. We have a tendency it seems to over complicate our lives and forget what's important and what's not. We tend to mistake movement for achievement. We tend to focus on activities instead of results. And as the pace of life continues to race along in the outside world, we forget that we have the power to control our lives regardless of what's going on outside."

-Robert Stuberg

OCT 22

"Your imagination, my dear fellow, is worth more than you imagine."

-Louis Aragon

OCT 23

"We think, sometimes, there's not a dragon left. Not one brave knight, not a single princess gliding through secret forests, enchanting deer and butterflies with her smile. What a pleasure to be wrong. Princesses, knights, enchantments and dragons, mystery and adventure ...not only are they here-and-now, they're all that ever lived on earth!"

-Richard Bach

OCT 24

"When I was a kid, I used to imagine animals running under my bed. I told my dad, and he solved the problem quickly. He cut the legs off the bed."

-Lou Brock

OCT 25

"All women should know how to take care of children. Most of them will have a husband some day."

-Franklin P. Jones

OCT 26

"Having children makes you no more a parent than having a piano makes you a pianist."

-Michael Levine

OCT 27

"Housework is a treadmill from futility to oblivion with stop-offs at tedium and counter productivity."

-Erma Bombeck

OCT 28

"Dusting is a good example of the futility of trying to put things right. As soon as you dust, the fact of your next dusting has already been established."

-George Carlin

OCT 29

"I noticed everyone makes a greater effort to hurt other people than to help himself."

-Alexis Carrel

OCT 30

"Integrity is not a 90 percent thing, not a 95 percent thing; either you have it or you don't."

-Peter Scotese

OCT 31

"Integrity without knowledge is weak and useless, and knowledge without integrity is dangerous and dreadful."

-Samuel Johnson

NOV 1

"Integrity is not a conditional word. It doesn't blow in the wind or change with the weather. It is your inner image of yourself, and if you look in there and see someone who won't cheat, then you know you never will."

-John D Macdonald

NOV 2

"Allow your children to fail if you want then to succeed."

Dr. Avril P. Beckford

NOV 3

"Look at a day when you are supremely satisfied at the end. It's not a day when you lounge around doing nothing; its when you had everything to do, and you've done it."

-Margaret Thatcher

NOV 4

"When you come to the end of all the light you know, and it's time to step into the darkness of the unknown, faith is knowing that one of two things shall happen: Either you will be given something solid to stand on or you will be taught to fly."

-Edward Teller

NOV 5

"Whatever you are from nature, keep to it; never desert your own line of talent...Be what Nature intended you for, and you will succeed; be anything else, and you will be ten thousand times worse than nothing."

-Sydney Smith

NOV 6

"The world is not respectable; it is mortal, tormented, confused, deluded forever; but it is shot through with beauty, with love, with glints of courage and laughter; and in these, the spirit blooms timidly, and struggles to the light amid the thorns."

-George Santayana

NOV 7

"I cannot believe that the purpose of life is to be happy. I think the purpose of life is to be useful, to be responsible, to be compassionate. It is, above all to matter, to count, to stand for something, to have made some difference that you lived at all."

-Leo Rosten

NOV 8

"Motivation is everything. You can do the work of two people, but you can't be two people. Instead, you have to inspire the next guy down the line and get him to inspire his people."

-Lee Iacocca

NOV 9

"Avoiding the phrase 'I don't have time...', will soon help you to realize that you do have the time needed for just about anything you choose to accomplish in life."

-Bo Bennett

NOV 10

"Leadership: The art of getting someone else to do something you want done because he wants to do it."

-Dwight D. Eisenhower

NOV 11

"He who has never learned to obey cannot be a good commander."

-Aristotle

NOV 12

"We are all motivated by a keen desire for praise, and the better a man is, the more he is inspired to glory."

-Cicero

NOV 13

"Any one can hold the helm when the sea is calm."

Publilius Syrus

NOV 14

"Nothing can stop the man with the right mental attitude from achieving his goal; nothing on earth can help the man with the wrong mental attitude."

-Thomas Jefferson

NOV 15

"There is only one success--to be able to spend your life in your own way."

-Christopher Morley

NOV 16

"It is easier to be wise for others than for ourselves."
-Francois De La Rochefoucauld

NOV 17

"One who understands much displays a greater simplicity of character than one who understands little."
-Alexander Chase

NOV 18

*"On every thorn, delightful wisdom grows,
In every rill a sweet instruction flows."*
-Edward Young

NOV 19

"Don't waste your life in doubts and fears: spend yourself on the work before you, well assured that the right performance of this hour's duties will be the best preparation for the hours or ages that follow it".
-Ralph Waldo Emerson

NOV 20

"Present fears are less than horrible imaginings."
-William Shakespeare

NOV 21

"Go back a little to leap further."
-John Clarke

NOV 22

"Our doubts are traitors, and make us lose the good we oft might win, by fearing to attempt."

-William Shakespeare

NOV 23

"Little minds are tamed and subdued by misfortunes; but great minds rise above them."

-Washington Irving

NOV 24

"It is the want of diligence, rather than the want of means, that causes most failures."

-Alfred Mercier

NOV 25

"When one door of happiness closes, another opens, but often we look so long at the closed door that we do not see the one that has been opened for us."

-Helen Keller

NOV 26

"Action may not always bring happiness; but there is no happiness without action."

Benjamin Disraeli

NOV 27

"Dost thou love life? Then do not squander time, for that is the stuff life is made of."

-Benjamin Franklin

NOV 28

"Most of the shadows of this life are caused by our standing in our own sunshine."

-Ralph Waldo Emerson

NOV 29

"After the game, the king and the pawn go into the same box."

-Italian Proverb

NOV 30

"We make our fortunes, and we call them fate."

-Earl of Beaconsfield

DEC 1

"As I grow to understand life less and less, I learn to love it more and more."

-Jules Renard

DEC 2

"To live is like to love--all reason is against it, and all healthy instinct for it."
-Samuel Butler

DEC 3

"Far away in the sunshine are my highest aspirations. I may not reach them, but I can look up and see their beauty, believe in them, and try to follow where they lead."
-Louisa May Alcott

DEC 4

"Your imagination is your preview of life's coming attractions."
-Albert Einstein

DEC 5

"The ability to convert ideas to things is the secret to outward success."
-Henry Ward Beecher

DEC 6

"Failures do what is tension relieving, while winners do what is goal achieving." -Dennis Waitley

DEC 7

"We can always redeem the man who aspires and strives."
-Johann Wolfgang von Goethe

DEC 8

"Every ceiling, when reached, becomes a floor, upon which one walks as a matter of course and prescriptive right."
-Aldous Huxley

DEC 9

"Winning isn't everything, but wanting to win is."
-Vince Lombardi

DEC 10

"Go confidently in the direction of your dreams. Live the life you have imagined."
-Henry David Thoreau

DEC 11

"The end of wisdom is to dream high enough not to lose the dream in the seeking of it."
-William Faulkner

DEC 12

"The fact is, that to do anything in the world worth doing, we must not stand back shivering and thinking of the cold and danger, but jump in and scramble through as well as we can."
-Robert Cushing

DEC 13

"Yes, know thyself: in great concerns or small, Be this thy care, for this, my friend, is all."
-Juvenal

DEC 14

"If we do not plant knowledge when young, it will give us no shade when we are old."
-Lord Chesterfield

DEC 15

"Collect as precious pearls the words of the wise and virtuous."
-Abd-el-Kadar

DEC 16

"Insist on yourself. Never imitate."
-Ralph Waldo Emerson

DEC 17

"In learning to know other things, and other minds, we become more intimately acquainted with ourselves, and are to ourselves better worth knowing."
-Philip Gilbert Hamilton

DEC 18

"A man who finds no satisfaction in himself will seek for it in vain elsewhere."
-La Rochefoucauld

DEC 19

*"No longer forward nor behind
I look in hope and fear;
But grateful take the good I find,
The best of now and here."*
-John G. Whittier

DEC 20

"It is idle to dread what you cannot avoid."
-Publius Syrus

DEC 21

"It is the trouble that never comes that causes the loss of sleep."
-Chas. Austin Bates

DEC 22

"A good deed is never lost: he who sows courtesy reaps friendship; and he who plants kindness gathers love."

-Basil

DEC 23

"Let us believe neither half of the good people tell us of ourselves, nor half of the evil they say of others."

-J. Petit Senn

DEC 24

"The less people speak of their greatness, the more we think of it."

-Lord Bacon

DEC 25

"The only thing bad about a holiday is it is followed by a non-holiday."

-Anon

DEC 26

"If we all worked on the assumption that what is accepted as true were really true, there would be little hope of advance."

-Orville Wright

DEC 27

"We always strive after what is forbidden, and desire the things refused us."
-Ovid

DEC 28

"We don't live in a world of reality, we live in a world of perceptions."
-Gerald J. Simmons

DEC 29

Happiness does not depend on outward things, but on the way we see them."
-Leo Tolstoy

DEC 30

"You cannot step twice into the same river, for other waters are continually flowing on."
-Heraclitus

DEC 31

"I demolish my bridges behind me...then there is no choice but to move forward."
-Firdtjof Nansen

Show appreciation to those who make your business grow!

Many companies are giving away this inspiring customizable book to say thank you to their:

New Customers
Loyal Customers
Dedicated Employees

*10% of proceeds are donated to the non-profit charity of your choice!**

Call Today!
866-443-6769

www.ErikaGilchrist.com

Orders of 50 or more, mention coupon code 1021 to receive a discount.

www.ingramcontent.com/pod-product-compliance
Lightning Source LLC
Chambersburg PA
CBHW061502040426
42450CB00008B/1452